Shifting in Keys for Violin

Book One:

Keys of C, G, D, F, and B♭

by Cassia Harvey

CHP256

©2014 by C. Harvey Publications All Rights Reserved.

www.charveypublications.com - print books & free sheet music blog
www.learnstrings.com - PDF downloadable books & chamber music

Half Steps in C Major

Cassia Harvey

The half steps in C major are between B and C and between E and F.
All of the other spaces between the notes in C major are whole steps.

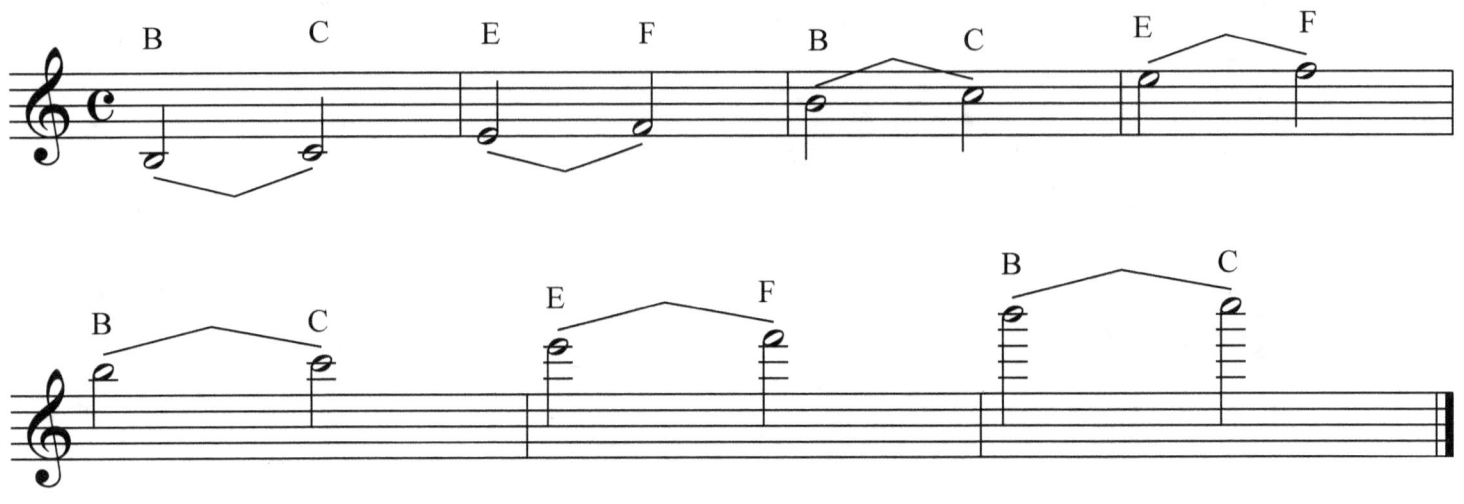

C Major Scale

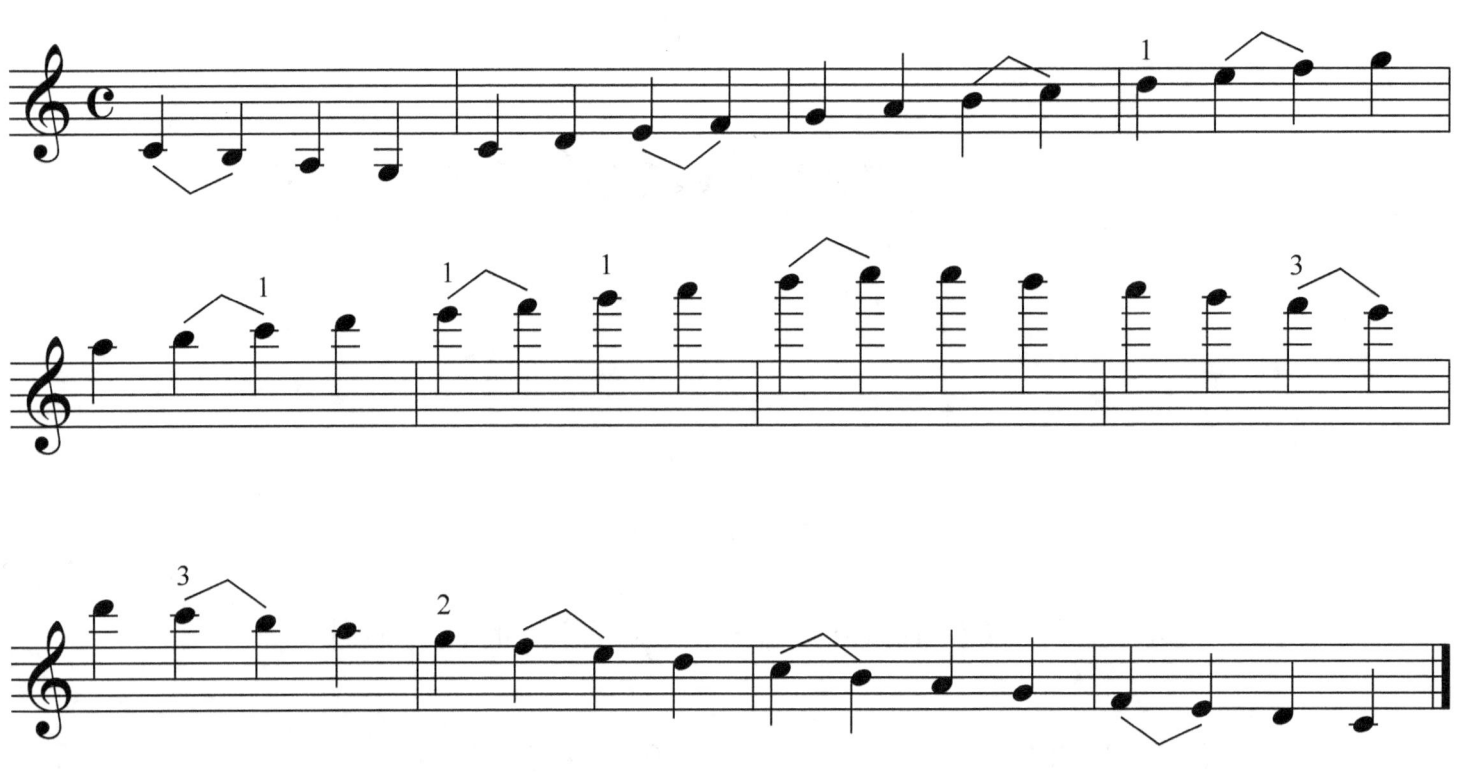

Shifting in Keys for Violin, Book One

C Major Study No. 1

©2014 C. Harvey Publications All Rights Reserved.

C Major Study No. 3

C Major Study No. 4

C Major Study No. 5

C Major Study No. 6

C Major Study No. 7

C Major Study No. 8

Shifting in Keys for Violin, Book One

C Major Study No. 9

Half Steps in G Major

The half steps in G major are between B and C and between F# and G.
All of the other spaces between the notes in G major are whole steps.

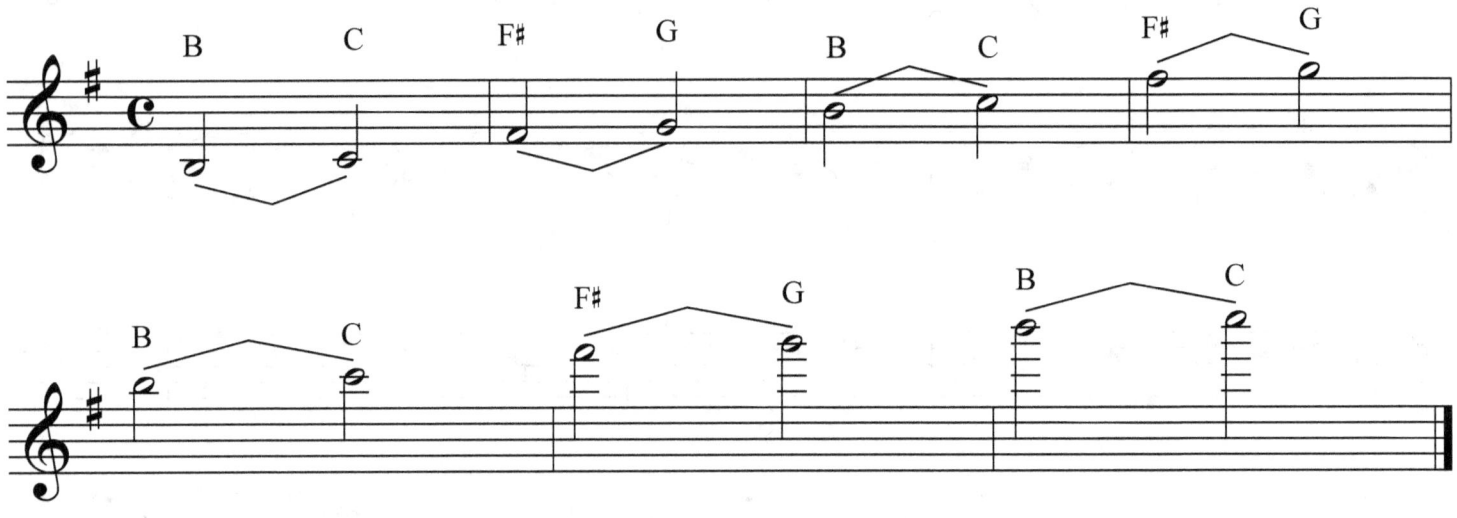

G Major Scale

G Major Study No. 1

G Major Study No. 2

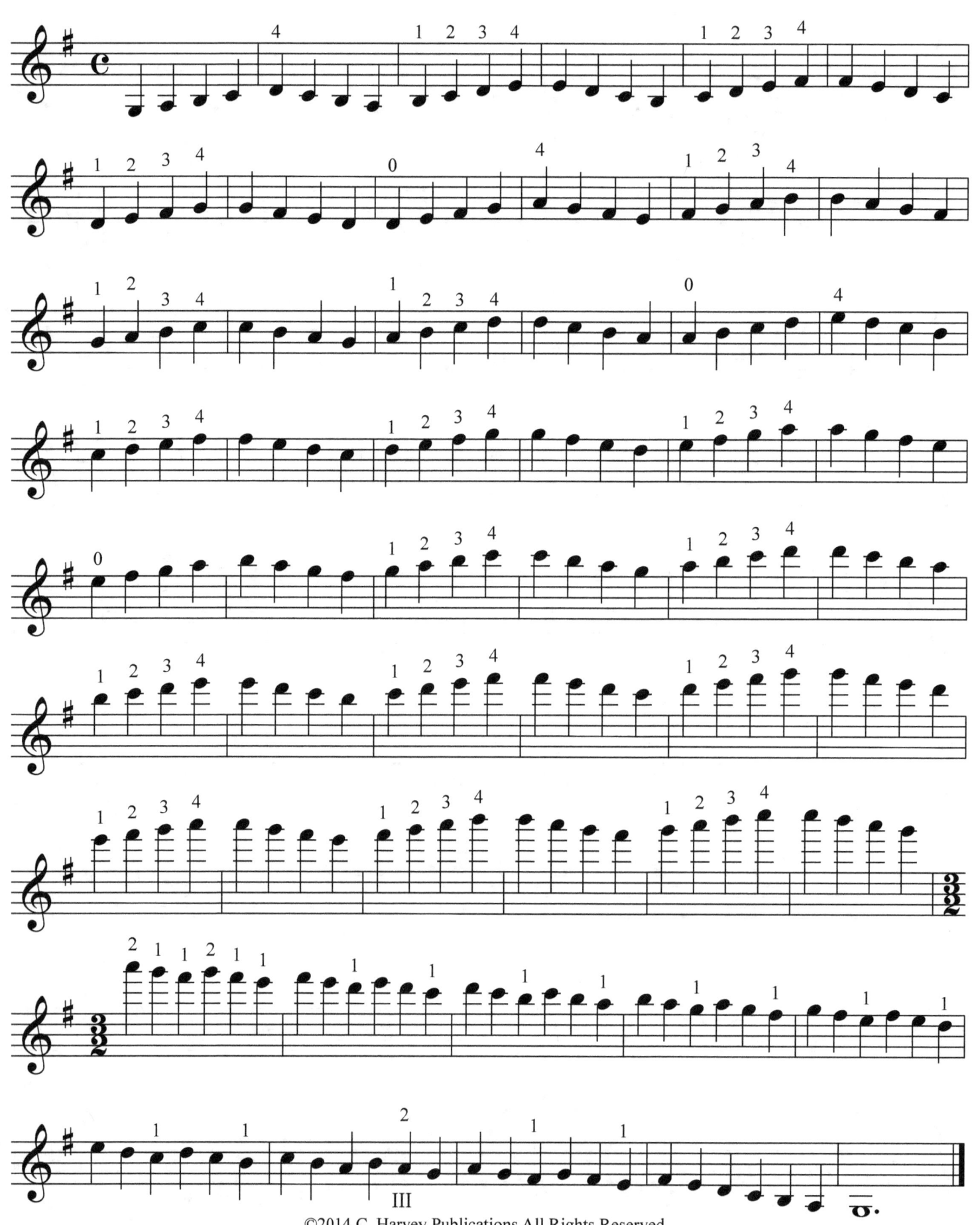

Shifting in Keys for Violin, Book One

G Major Study No. 3

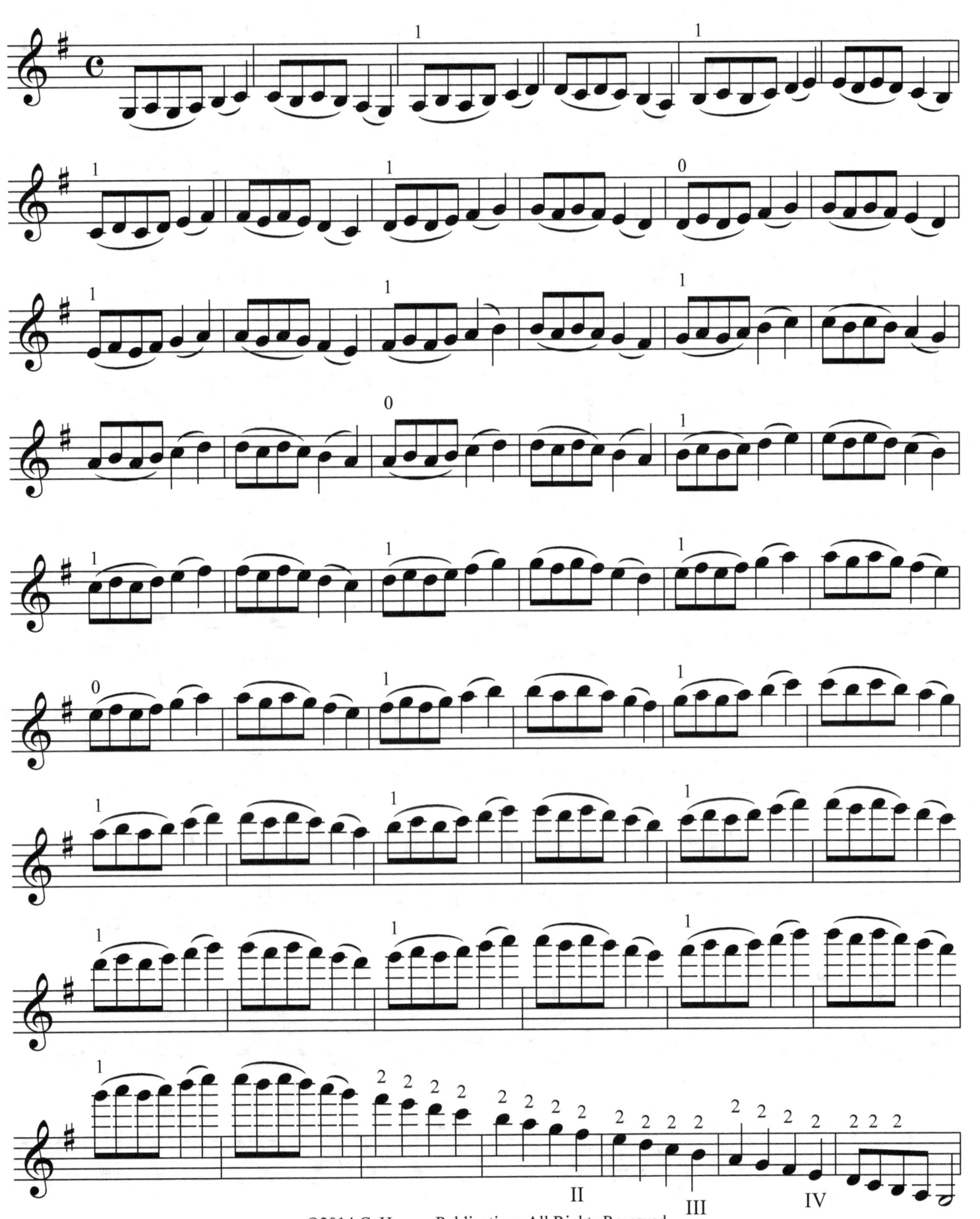

©2014 C. Harvey Publications All Rights Reserved.

G Major Study No. 4

Shifting in Keys for Violin, Book One

Shifting in Keys for Violin, Book One

G Major Study No. 5

G Major Study No. 6

Shifting in Keys for Violin, Book One

G Major Study No. 7

G Major Study No. 8

Shifting in Keys for Violin, Book One

©2014 C. Harvey Publications All Rights Reserved.

G Major Study No. 9

Shifting in Keys for Violin, Book One

Half Steps in D Major

The half steps in D major are between C♯ and D and between F♯ and G.
All of the other spaces between the notes in D major are whole steps.

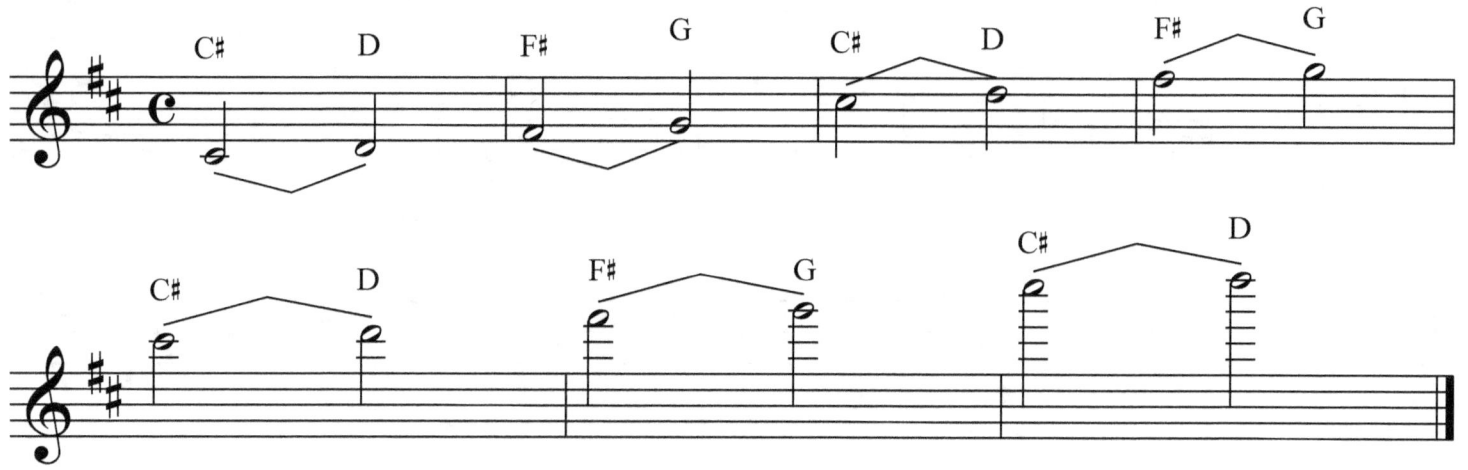

D Major Scale

D Major Study No. 1

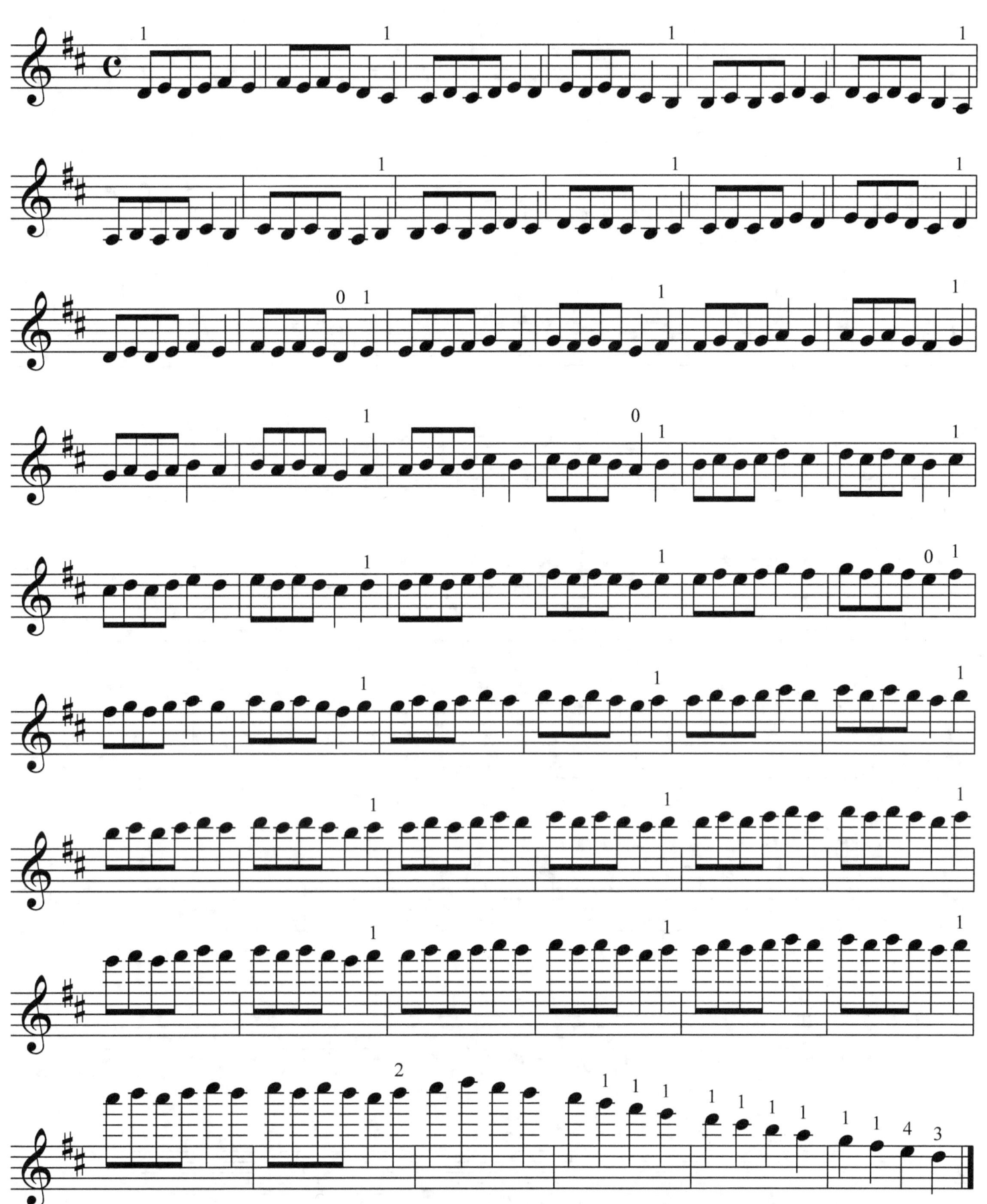

D Major Study No. 2

D Major Study No. 3

Shifting in Keys for Violin, Book One

D Major Study No. 4

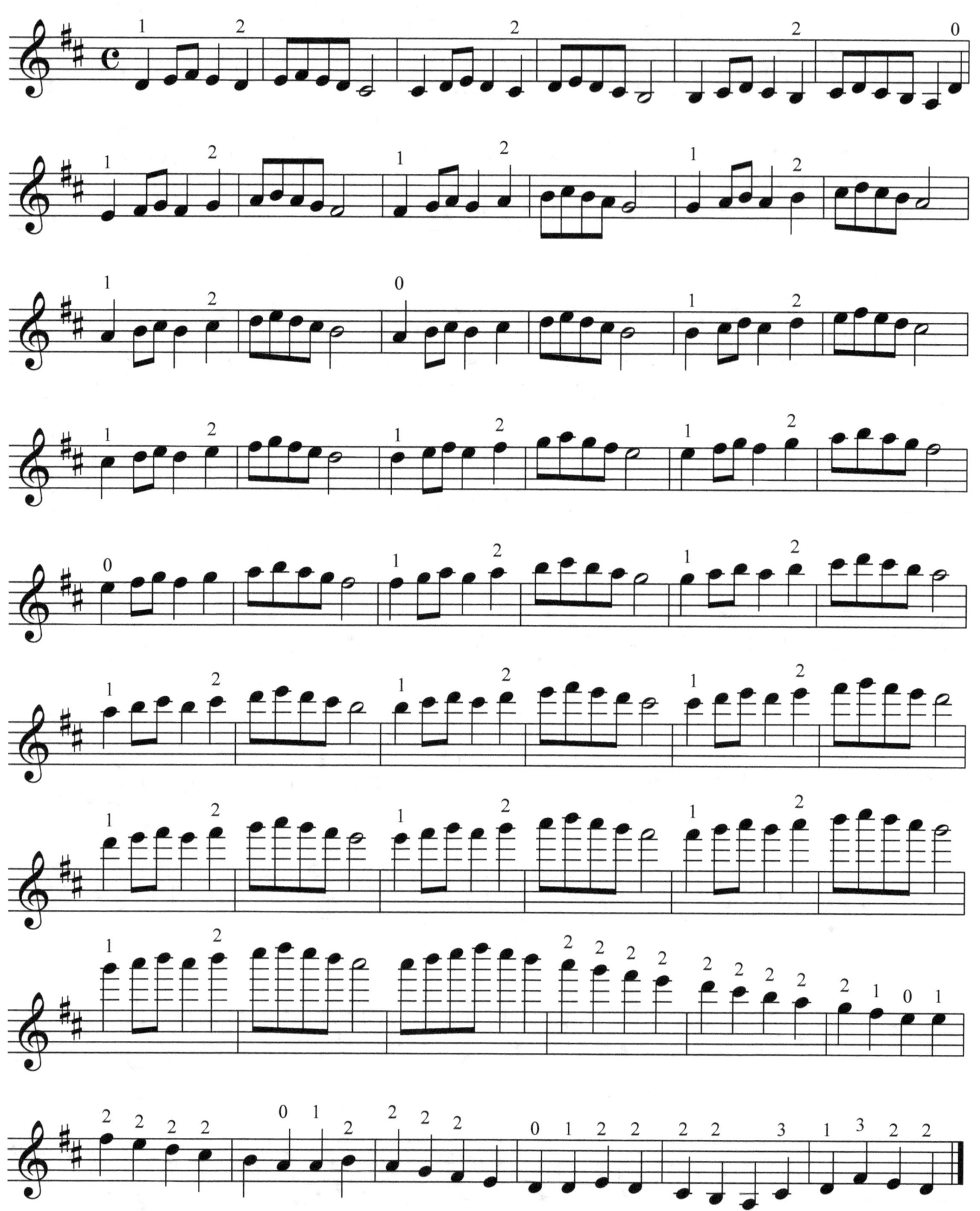

D Major Study No. 5

Shifting in Keys for Violin, Book One

©2014 C. Harvey Publications All Rights Reserved.

D Major Study No. 6

Shifting in Keys for Violin, Book One

D Major Study No. 7

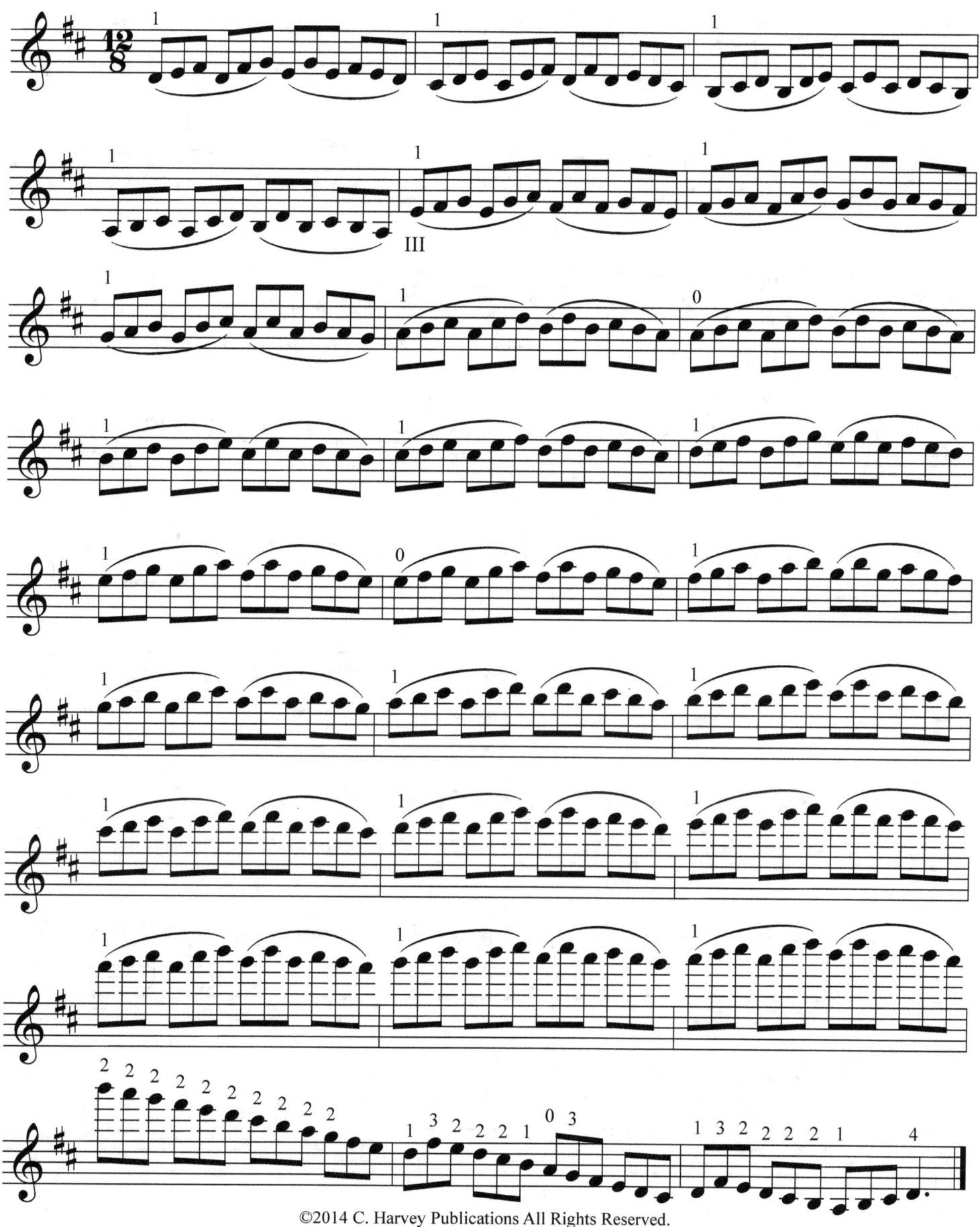

D Major Study No. 8

D Major Study No. 9

Half Steps in F Major

The half steps in F major are between A and B♭ and between E and F.
All of the other spaces between the notes in F major are whole steps.

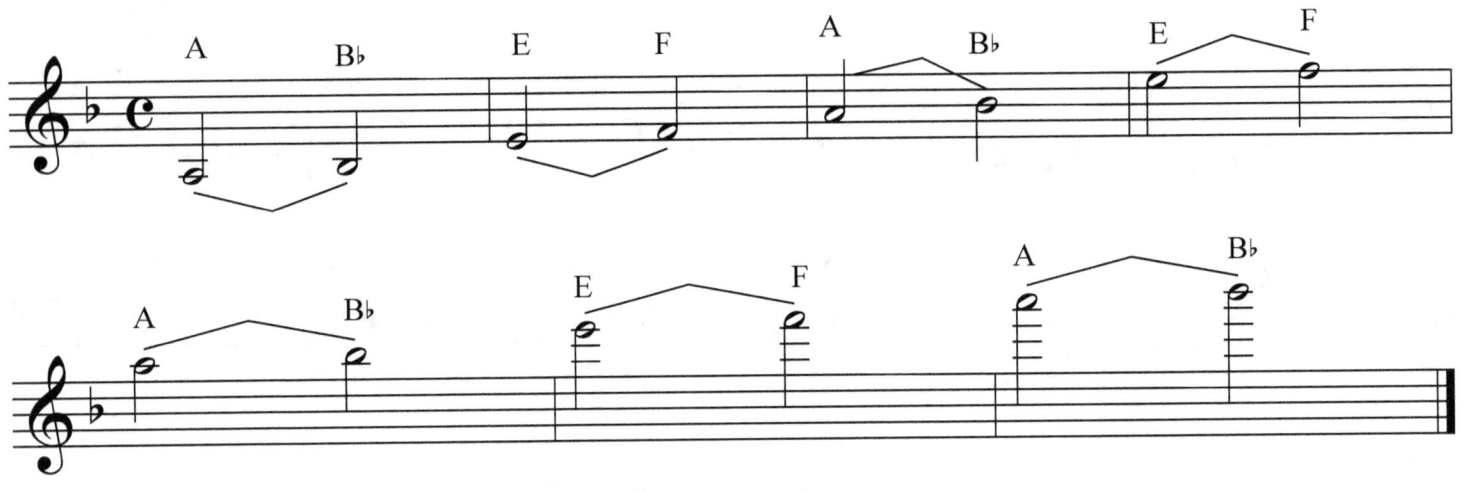

F Major Scale

F Major Study No. 1

F Major Study No. 2

Shifting in Keys for Violin, Book One

©2014 C. Harvey Publications All Rights Reserved.

F Major Study No. 3

F Major Study No. 4

Shifting in Keys for Violin, Book One

©2014 C. Harvey Publications All Rights Reserved.

F Major Study No. 5

Shifting in Keys for Violin, Book One

F Major Study No. 6

F Major Study No. 7

Shifting in Keys for Violin, Book One

©2014 C. Harvey Publications All Rights Reserved.

F Major Study No. 8

Shifting in Keys for Violin, Book One

F Major Study No. 9

©2014 C. Harvey Publications All Rights Reserved.

Half Steps in B♭ Major

The half steps in B♭ major are between A and B♭ and between D and E♭.
All of the other spaces between the notes in B♭ major are whole steps.

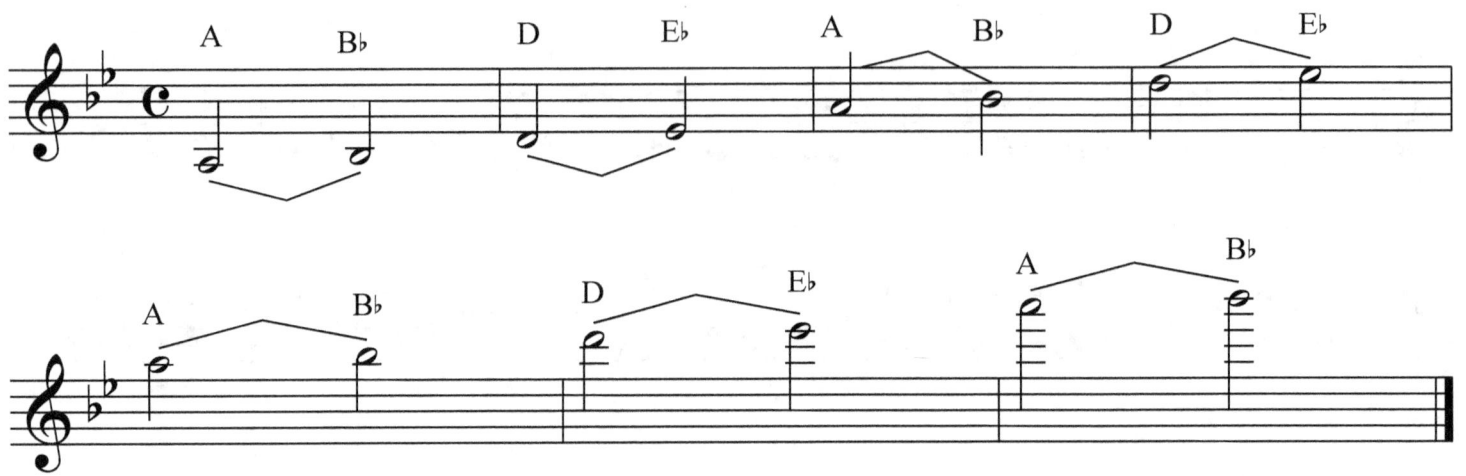

B♭ Major Scale

Shifting in Keys for Violin, Book One

B♭ Major Study No. 1

B♭ Major Study No. 2

B♭ Major Study No. 3

B♭ Major Study No. 4

Shifting in Keys for Violin, Book One

B♭ Major Study No. 5

©2014 C. Harvey Publications All Rights Reserved.

B♭ Major Study No. 6

B♭ Major Study No. 7

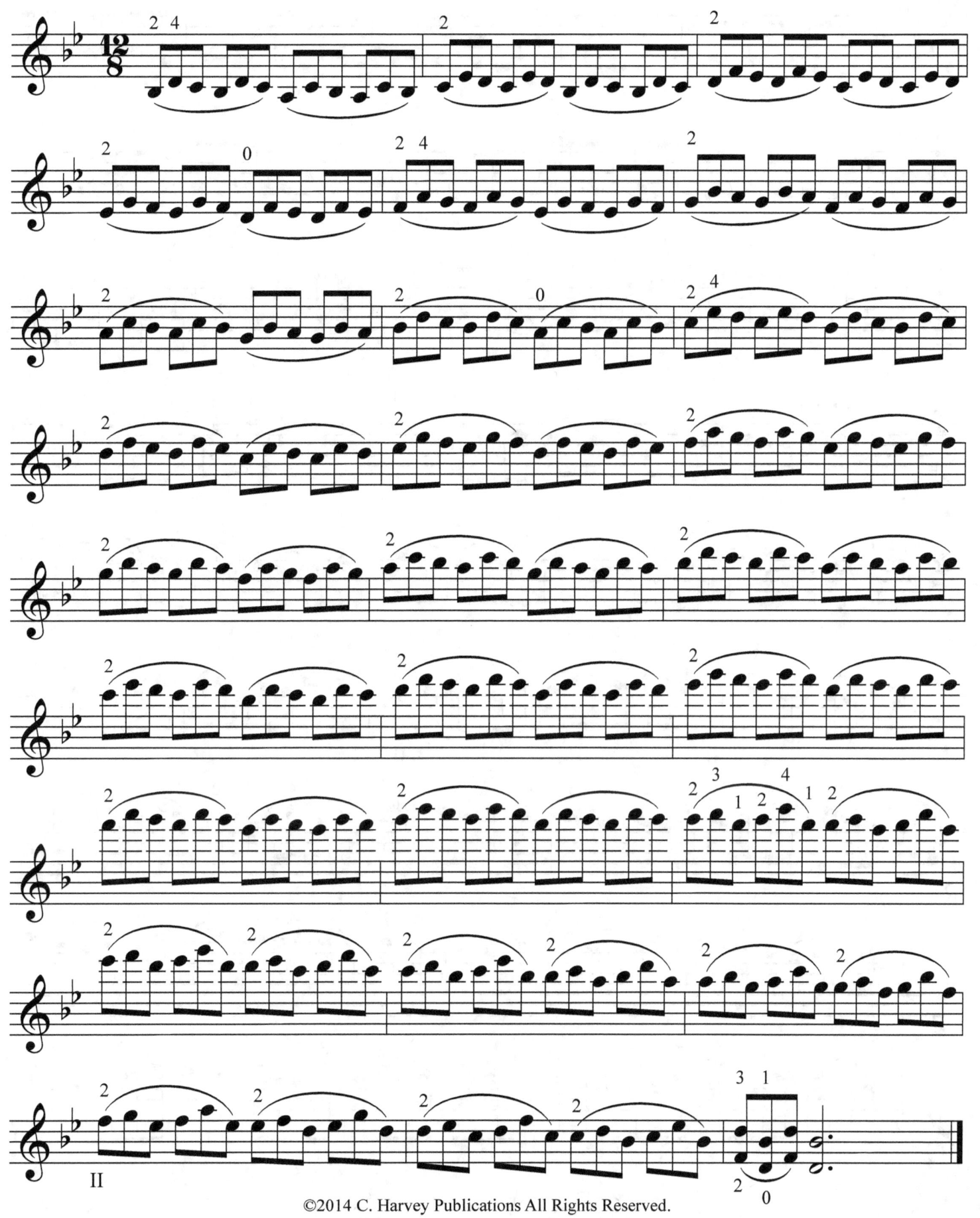

B♭ Major Study No. 8

Shifting in Keys for Violin, Book One

©2014 C. Harvey Publications All Rights Reserved.

Shifting in Keys for Violin, Book One

B♭ Major Study No. 9

©2014 C. Harvey Publications All Rights Reserved.